HOW TO BUILD YOUR OWN DOLL'S HOUSE

USING PAPER AND CARDBOARD

—

STEP-BY-STEP INSTRUCTIONS ON
CONSTRUCTING A DOLL'S HOUSE, INDOOR
AND OUTDOOR FURNITURE, FIGURINES,
UTENCILS AND MORE

—

BY
E. V. LUCAS
AND
E. LUCAS

British Library Cataloguing-in-Publication Data
A catalogue record for this book is available from the
British Library

E. V. Lucas

Edward Verrall Lucas was born in Eltham, England in 1868. In his youth, he worked in bookshops and newspaper offices, before rising to the senior staff of *Punch Magazine* in 1904. Over the rest of his life, Lucas was a prolific writer, producing almost a hundred books and providing much content for *Punch* and a number of national newspapers. He wrote extensively on cricket – his collection, *Cricket All His Life,* is considered one of the best books on cricket of all time – as well as politics, current affairs, travel and the arts. Lucas is particularly remembered for his biography of the notable English essayist Charles Lamb. He died in 1938, aged 70.

THIS · BOOK · IS · THE · PROPERTY · OF ·

Dollhouses

A dollhouse or doll's house is often a toy home, made in miniature. For the last century, dollhouses have primarily been the domain of children but their collection and crafting is also a hobby for many adults. Dollhouses can range from the amateur miniaturist placing a few decorated boxes on top of one another to be enjoyed by one person, up to incomparable multi-million dollar structures viewed by millions of people each year. Today's children's dollhouses originally originated from the *baby house* display cases of sixteenth century Europe, designed to show idealised interiors. Smaller dollhouses with more realistic exteriors appeared in Europe in the eighteenth century. Early dollhouses were all handmade, but following the Industrial Revolution and the Second World War, they were increasingly mass-produced and became more standardized and affordable.

Miniature homes, furnished with domestic articles and resident inhabitants, both people and animals, have been made for thousands of years. The earliest known examples were found in the Egyptian tombs of the Old Kingdom, created nearly five thousand years ago. These wooden representations found in the Pyramids, including models of servants, furnishings, boats, livestock and pets were almost certainly were made for religious purposes. But the earliest known European dollhouses appeared in the sixteenth century. They were each handmade and unique, and consisted of cabinet display cases made up of individual rooms. A prime example of the genre is Duke Albrecht V of Bavaria's realistic, yet miniature copy of his royal residence in 1557. Most other dollhouses of this period showed idealised interiors complete with extremely detailed furnishings and accessories. It should be pointed out that such items were solely intended as the play things of adults; they were an expression of status and wealth, very far from a children's toy. Fully furnished, such models were worth the price of a modest-full-size house's construction.

Smaller doll houses such as the 'Tate house', with more realistic exteriors, appeared in Europe in the eighteenth century. Germany was the producer of the most prized dollhouses and doll house miniatures up until the First World War, and notable German companies included Märklin, Rock and Graner, and others. Their products were not only avidly collected in Central Europe, but regularly exported to Britain and North America. After the War, Germany's dire financial and industrial situation impeded both production and export, and she ceased to be the main producer of dollhouses. Post-World War Two, dollhouses began to be mass-produced on a much larger scale than previously, with notably less detailed craftsmanship. By the 1950s, a typical commercial dollhouse was made of painted sheet metal filled with plastic furniture. Such houses were inexpensive enough that the great majority of girls from developed countries (those not struggling with rebuilding after the war) could own one.

Today, there are dozens of miniature trade shows held each year by various miniature organisations and enthusiasts. Here, artisans and dealers display and sell miniatures to others in the trade, as well as the public. Often, how-to seminars and workshops, for those keen to 'build their own' are part of the show features. There are also numerous internet forums, blogs and other online-social medias concentrated solely on dollhouses and miniatures. Some miniatures are true treasures worth hundreds of thousands of dollars, with a rare few dating back thousands of years. Current children's dollhouses are commonly 1:18 scale, whereas the most common standard for adult collectors is 1:12 scale.

There are three major museum quality palatial dollhouses in the world, where this art form has been taken to the highest calibre: Queen Mary's Dolls' House; the Dollhouse of Colleen Moore; and Astolat Dollhouse Castle. Each can weigh up to 2,000 pounds, appraise at well over a million pounds, and contain furnishings that are as true-to-life as humanly possible. However, as an interesting note, one of the things that you will never see in the interiors of these world-class dollhouses, is a doll. The inability to precisely replicate the human body and face in miniature would detract from the accuracy of these perfect miniature settings. Queen Mary's Dolls' House is part of the Royal Collection Trust and is on show at Windsor Castle, England. When first put on display it was visited by 1.6 million people in seven months. Moore's dollhouse is called the 'Fairy Castle' and would cost over £7 million if built today. It is visited by an estimated 1.5 million people each year where it resides in Chicago at the Museum of Industry and Science. The Astolat Dollhouse Castle is on display at the Nassau County Museum of Art on Long Island, New York. All were built to 1:12 scale, although they vary in overall size. The Queen Mary's Dolls' House is approximately 5' tall, contains 16 rooms, and required 4 years to construct. The Colleen Moore dollhouse is 7' tall, has twelve rooms, and took 7 years to construct. The Astolat Castle Dollhouse is 9' tall, has 29 rooms, and required more than 10 years to build. We hope the reader enjoys this book on dollhouses, and is inspired to create their own (perhaps more modest!) miniature dwelling.

DOLLS' HOUSES

DOLLS' HOUSES

THE most magnificent ready-made dolls' house in the world, with gables and windows, stairs, front garden, and the best furniture, cannot quite make up to its owner for all the delight she has missed by not making it herself. Of course some things, such as cups and saucers, glasses and bottles, saucepans and kitchen utensils, must be bought ; but almost all the really necessary things for housekeeping can be made at home.

One advantage of making the dolls' house yourself is that *Dolls'* you can arrange for it to have a garden, a provision rarely made *garden.* by toy-shops. Grass plots can be made of green baize or other cloth of the right colour ; garden paths of sand sprinkled over gum, or of strips of sand-paper ; flower-beds of brown paper, and the flowers of tissue-paper and wire. A summer-house, and a dog-kennel to hold a china dog, might also be added (see p. 197), and, if you have room, stables.

Garden seats and tables can be made of cardboard and[27] *t. Garden* For a seat, take a card two or three inches long and not quite *chairs* as broad. Mark it right across, lengthwise, in the middle with a *tables.* sharp knife, and then half fold it. This will make the back and seat. Gum, or seccotine, the seat to four slender corks for legs and paint the whole green. To make a table, gum or press four cork legs to a strong piece of cardboard.

A dolls' house can be made of almost any kind of box. For *The ho* the simplest and smallest kind cigar boxes can be used, and the

N

furniture made of cork, for which directions are given later ; or a couple of low shelves in a bookcase or cupboard will do. Much better, however, is a large well-made packing-case divided by wooden and strong cardboard partitions into two, four, or six rooms, according to its size. A specially made box is, of course, best of all ; this should be divided into four or six rooms, and should have a sloping roof to give attic-room for boxes and odd furniture. The house can be stained outside or papered a plain dark colour. One or two windows should be cut out of the walls of each room by the carpenter who made the box, and there must be doors between the rooms. A piece of thin glass cut to the right size can be fixed on the windows at home. But before this is done the house must be papered. The best kind of paper is that used by bookbinders for the insides of the covers, because the patterns used are so dainty and small ; but this is not always easy to get. Any small-patterned paper will do, or what is called lining paper, which can be got in every colour. The paper must be very smoothly put on with paste. Always start at the top when pressing it to the wall, and smooth it downwards gently. Dadoes or friezes can be divided off with the tiny beading which frame-makers use, or with a painted line, which must be straight and evenly done.

Fireplaces, which can be bought or made at home, should be put in next. To make one yourself, take a strong cardboard-box lid about four inches long and two wide (though the size must depend on the size of the room). Very neatly cut off a quarter of it. This smaller part, covered with gold or silver paper, will make the fender. Then cut off both sides of the remaining piece, leaving the strip at the top to form the mantelpiece. Glue the back of the cover to the wall, hang little curtains from the shelf, put some ornaments on it, arrange the fender in front, and the fireplace is complete. A grate can be imitated in cardboard painted black and red. Gelatine cracker-paper will make an excellent glowing fire.

A splendid game of shop can be played while the furnishing *A furr*
is going on ; in fact, from the moment you have the bare house *ing ga*
a board or sign with "*To be Let or Sold*" will quickly attract
house-hunting dolls, and when a couple have taken it they will
have their days full of shopping before it is ready for them.
You will, of course, yourself be the manufacturers and shop-
keepers. It is well to make out careful bills for everything sold,
and the more things you can display in your show-rooms the
better. All house-hunting dolls require plenty of money.
Windows have been mentioned, but they are not by any *Curtai*
means a necessity. Yet even if you cannot have windows, you
should put up curtains, for they make the rooms prettier. Blinds
can be made of linen, edged at the bottom with a piece of lace,
and nailed on the wall just above the window. During the
day these are rolled up and tied. White curtains should be
bordered with lace and run on a piece of tape, which can be
nailed or pinned on both sides of the window. They will then
draw. The stuff curtains can be hung on a pencil (which may
be gilded or left its own colour) supported by two picture screws.
Fasten these curtains back with narrow ribbons. Some dolls'
houses, of course, are fitted with real doors. But if you do not
have these, it is perhaps well to hang the doorway with curtains,
also on pencils.
The floors can be stained or painted either all over or round *Floors.*
the edges. Carpets are better not made of ordinary carpet, for
it is much too thick, but of coloured canvas, or chintz, or thin
felt, or serge. A rug made of a plain coloured material with a
cross-stitch or embroidered pattern around it is very pretty.
Fine matting can also be used, and American cloth is excellent
for the kitchen.
In another place in this book (pp. 185-190) will be found *Genera*
instructions for making furniture for very small and simple dolls' *remark*
houses ; but for a good dolls' house 9 - 14 *veral* good-sized *furnisle*
rooms you would probably prefer, for the most part, to use

3

bought things. Square tables are of course easy to make (a cardboard-box lid on four legs is practically the whole thing), and there are other articles which, if you see your way to devise, are better made at home, instructions for which will be found as you read on ; but chairs and round tables and so forth are perhaps most satisfactory when they come from the toy-shop. Both in buying furniture and in making it, it is necessary always to remember the size of the rooms and of the dolls, and the size of whatever furniture you may already have, so as to keep everything in proportion.

Beds can be made of cardboard boxes of different sizes. The box turned upside down makes the bed itself, and the cover should

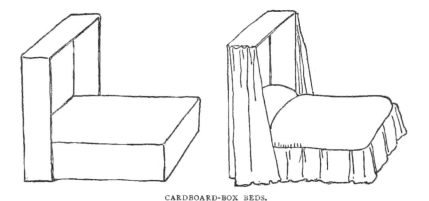

CARDBOARD-BOX BEDS.

be fixed upright behind it for curtains to hang from. These curtains and the frill round the bed should be made of any thin material, such as muslin. The mattress, bolster, and pillows are best made of cotton-wool covered with muslin or calico. Sheets may be made also out of muslin ; pillow-cases should be edged with lace ; for blankets you use flannel, button-hole-stitched round with coloured silk or wool, and the quilt will look

4

best if made of a dainty piece of silk, or muslin over a coloured sateen to match the curtains. A tiny nightdress case should not be forgotten. Beds for doll children can be made in the same way out of match-boxes; and for cosy little cots for babies there are walnut shells

Chairs can be made with wire, beads, a little silk or cotton *Bead* material, some cardboard and cotton-wool. To make a chair in *furni*this way, cut a piece of cardboard the size that you want the seat

BEAD CHAIR.

to be. Lay a good wad of cotton-wool over it, and then cover it neatly. On a piece of strong wire thread enough beads to go round the seat of the chair. Sew this firmly to the seat. Then thread beads on four pieces of wire the right length for the legs, and leave a little piece of wire with which to fasten them to the wire round the seat. Then make the back from a longer piece of wire, bent into shape and attached to the seat in the same way, and put a short row of beads across the middle. You will need a pair of tweezers to cut the wire and to finish the fastening securely.

Pictures for the walls can be made very easily. The picture *Pictu*itself will be a scrap or tiny photograph. This is pasted on a

5

piece of cardboard larger than itself, and round the edge of that you place a strip of whatever coloured paper you want for the frame. The picture cord, a piece of cotton, can be fastened on the back with stamp paper. More elaborate frames are cut out of cardboard and bound round with coloured silk and covered with gold paint. The picture is then stuck into it.

shelves *ooks.* The simplest bookshelves are those that hang from a nail on the wall. They are made by cutting two or three strips of cardboard of the size of the shelves and boring holes at the corners of

HANGING BOOKSHELVES.

each. These are then threaded one by one on four lengths of silk or fine string, knots being tied to keep the shelves the right distance apart, as in the drawing. Care has to be taken to get the knots exactly even, or the shelf will be crooked.

Books can be made by sewing together a number of tiny sheets of paper, with a coloured cover and a real or invented title. Sometimes these books contain real stories.

es. A dolls' house ought to be as complete as possible, and though this will take a long time it is absorbingly interesting work from start to finish. It should be the ambition of the mistress of a dolls' house to have it as well furnished as the house of a grown-up person, and if she looks round the rooms in her own

6

home carefully she will see how many things can be copied. There will be cushions to make, fancy table-cloths for different tables, toilet-covers and towels for the bedroom, splashers to go behind washstands, mats in front of them, and roll-towels and kitchen cloths for the kitchen.

Everything should be made of the thinnest and finest material, cut with the greatest care and sewn with the tiniest stitches. Light and dainty colours are best for a dolls' house. If you have several rooms, it is a good plan to have a pink room, a blue room, a yellow room, and in each room to have everything of different shades of that colour and white. Perhaps no material is so useful to the owner of a dolls' house as art muslin. It is soft, cheap, and very pretty.

Coming to other furniture which can be made at home, we find screens (made of cardboard and scraps), music for the piano, walking-sticks, flowers (made of coloured tissue-paper and wire), flower-pots (made of corks covered with red paper), cupboards to keep linen and glass in (made out of small cardboard boxes, fitted with shelves), and many other little things which, if you look round your own home carefully, will be suggested to you. Even bicycles can be imitated in cardboard and placed in the hall.

As to dolls, the more the merrier. They are so cheap and *The* can be dressed so easily that it seems a great pity not to have a *inhabi* large family and a larger circle of friends who will occasionally visit them. There must be a father and a mother, a baby and some children, servants (in stiff print dresses with caps and aprons), and certainly a bride, who, if her dress cannot be changed for an ordinary one, ought to be kept carefully hidden, except when there is a wedding.

It is rather difficult to dress these tiny dolls so that their *Dressi* clothes will take off and on, but it is much better to do so if *dolls.* possible. In any case they can have capes and hats which take off. The thinnest materials make the best under-clothes, but stiff material for dresses makes it possible to stand the dolls up.

Glove buttons, and the narrowest ribbons, tapes, and laces, are useful things to have when you are dressing dolls'-house dolls.

' dinner
'es.

Dolls occasionally require parties. The food may be real or imitation. If real,—such as currants and raisins, sugar and candied peel,—it is more amusing at the moment ; but if imitation, you have a longer time of interest in making it. Get a little flour, and mix it with salt and water into a stiff paste, like clay. Then mould it to resemble a round of beef, a chicken, a leg of mutton, potatoes, pies, or whatever you want, and stand it in front of the fire to dry. When dry, paint (in water-colour) to resemble these things still more. If there is clay in the garden, you can make all these things from that, and many others too.

' flats.

Just as people live not only in houses but in flats, so may there be dolls' flats as well as dolls' houses. A dolls' flat consists of a board on which the outline of the rooms is made with single bricks. For example, a four-roomed flat might be arranged like this—

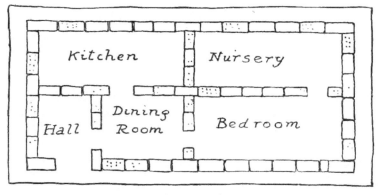

A DOLLS' FLAT.

To lay the bricks on a board is not necessary. They can be laid on the floor equally well, except that when you have done playing

8

you will have then to put them away again, whereas if placed on a board they can be left till next time. Nor is there any reason why the walls should not be higher than a single brick ; that is merely a matter of taste. Once the walls are ready the furniture and dolls can be put in in the ordinary way.

SMALLER DOLLS' HOUSES

So far we have been considering larger dolls' houses. But *Smalle* there are also smaller ones, which naturally require much smaller *dolls' h*

ARM-CHAIR, CORK (see p. 186).

furniture. These dolls' houses can be 10 ide of cardboard (as described on p. 193 and on), or they can be merely small boxes—even cigar boxes ; and the dolls and furniture in them can be, if you like, all 𝔣 17 ⁚, or made of materials in ways that are now suggested.

This furniture, if very neatly made, can be very successful, and *Cork a* it costs almost nothing. Plain pins will do quite well, although *match-* the fancy ones are much prettier. Velvet or thin cloth is best for *furnitu* the dining-room furniture ; silk for the drawing-room ; and some light-coloured cotton material for the bedrooms.

You will need—

Several good-sized corks, or pickle corks, for the larger things.
Some pieces of fancy silk or velvet.
A number of strong pins of different sizes. (The fancy pins with large white, black, and coloured heads are best.)
Some wool, silk, or tinsel which will go well with the silk or velvet.
A strong needle and a reel of cotton.

Cut a round or square piece of cork about quarter of an inch thick and one inch across. Cover it with a piece of silk or velvet, making all the stitches on that side of the cork which will be the under side of the seat. For the legs put a pin firmly into each corner. Wind a little wool or silk firmly round each leg, finishing it off as neatly as possible. The back of the seat is made by sticking four pins rather closely together and winding the wool or silk in and out of them. Fasten the wool with a tiny knot both when you begin winding and when you finish. Arm-chairs are made in the same way, except that they are rather larger, and arms—made of small pins—are added.

Very good dining-room chairs can be made of chestnuts. The flatter side of the nut is the seat, and in this are stuck pins for the back (and arms if necessary), which may be bound together with gold or silver tinsel. Other pins are stuck in underneath for legs.

For a sofa a piece of cork about two inches long and half an inch thick is needed. This must be covered, and then quite short pins stuck in for legs. Put a row of short pins along one side and the two ends, and wind the wool neatly in and out of them.

Round tables can be made best of different-sized pieces of cork, with very strong pins for legs ; and square ones of the outside of a wooden match-box, with four little medicine-bottle corks gummed under it for legs. In either case it is most important to have the legs well fixed on and of exactly the same length. It is not necessary to cover a table, but a table-cloth of silk, either fringed, or hemmed with tiny stitches, and a white table-cloth for meals, should be made.

10

Fancy tables can be made by taking a flat round cork and sticking pins into it at regular intervals all round. Weave silk or tinsel in and out of the pins until they are covered. (See below.)

Several small pieces of cork may be covered to make foot- *Foot-sto* stools.

CHESTNUT CHAIR (see p. 186).

A serviceable standard lamp can be made by taking a small *Standar* empty cotton reel, gilding or painting it,[10] and fixing the wooden *lamp.*

FANCY TABLE (see above).

part of a thin penholder firmly into it. On the top of it gum a round piece of cork, on which a lamp-shade, made of one of the little red paper caps that chemists put on bottles, can be placed.

BEDROOM FURNITURE

erials

You will need—

Two large wooden match-boxes.

Several corks of different sizes.

Some pieces of chintz, of cotton material, flannel, linen, American cloth, and a little cotton-wool.

An empty walnut shell.

Several wooden matches with the heads taken off.

Pins of different sizes.

Wool, silk or tinsel, for the backs of the chairs.

A tube of seccotine or some very strong gum.

To make a bed, take the inside of a match-box and cut away the bottom of it. Then take two matches and gum them to the two corners at the head of the bed so that a portion sticks out

MATCH-BOX BEDSTEAD.

below the bed for legs and above the bed for a railing. Cut two more matches to the same length as these others, less the part of them that serves for legs, and fasten these at equal distances from each other and from the two others already gummed in position. Along the top of these place another match for a rail, and the head of the bed is done. For the foot of the bed repeat these

12

operations exactly, except that all the upright matches must be a little shorter. Then cut off one end of the bottom of the box and fit it in to form the part of the bed that takes the mattress. It can be fastened in with stamp-paper. The bedstead, when made, should be like the one in the accompanying picture. A little mattress must now be made to fit the bed exactly ; it can be stuffed with cotton-wool or bran. A pillow, blankets, sheets, and a fancy coverlet may also be made, and a very thin and tiny frill should be put right round the bed to hide the box.

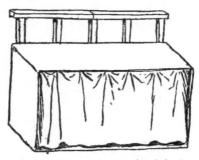

MATCH-BOX WASHSTAND (see below).

A very pretty baby's cradle can be made out of half a walnut shell. It should be lined, and curtains should be hung from a match fastened upright at one end of the shell.

The outside of the same match-box that was used for the *Dress*- bed will make a dressing-table. Stand it up on either of its *tables.* striking sides, and gum or sew a piece of light-coloured thin material all round it, and then over this put a muslin frill. Make a little white cloth to lay on the top of the table. The looking-glass is made by fixing a square of silver paper in a cardboard frame.

Take the inside of another match-box and stand it up on one *Wash* of its sides. Then take five or six matches and cut them to *stands* that length which, when they are gummed in an upright row at

13

equal distances apart to the back of the match-box, will cause them to stand up above the top of it about a third of an inch. On the tops of them then lay another match to make a little railing. Cover the box as you did the dressing-table. Put a little mat of American cloth on the top of the box, and

TOWEL-HORSE.

CLOTHES-BASKET.

make another large one to lay in front of it. Proper jugs and basins will, of course, have to be bought, but an acorn cup or small shell makes a very good toy basin.

drobes.   The wardrobe is made by standing the inside of a match-box on end, fixing inside several little pegs made of small pieces of match stuck in with seccotine, and hanging two little curtains in front of it. If, when done, it seems too low, it may be raised on four little corks.

el-horse.   A towel-horse can easily be made with six long pins and two small pieces of cork.

hes-   To make a clothes-basket, take a round piece of cork about
t. a quarter of an inch thick and stick pins closely together all round it, as in the above picture. Then weave wool in and out of them.

14

DOLLS' HOUSES AND DOLLS OF
CARDBOARD AND PAPER

DOLLS' HOUSES AND DOLLS OF CARDBOARD AND PAPER

A CARDBOARD house, furnished with paper furniture and occupied by paper dolls, is a very good substitute for an ordinary dolls' house, and the making of it is hardly less interesting. The simplest way to make a cardboard house is to cut it all (with the exception of the partition and the roof) in one piece.

The plan given here is for a two-roomed cottage, the measurements for which can be multiplied to whatever size you like (or whatever is the utmost that your sheet of cardboard will permit). The actual model from which this plan was made (the house was built from a royal sheet of Bristol board) had a total floor measurement of 8 inches by 14. The end walls were 5 inches high, the side walls 5 inches, sloping up to 7 in the middle, and the partition was 7 inches. The roof was slightly wider than the floor, in order to make wide eaves, and as much longer as was needful not only for the eaves but also to allow for the angle.

The first thing to do is to rule the outline of the cottage. All the measurements must be most accurately made, as the slightest incorrectness will keep the house from fitting together properly. Then cut it out. When this is done, draw the windows and doors. Then lay your cardboard on a board, and run your knife along each side of the windows and the three free sides of the doors until the card is cut through. A ruler held

O

close to the pencilled line will make your knife cut straight. The bars across the windows can be made of strips of paper gummed on afterwards. If the doors have a tiny piece shaved off each of the cut sides, they will open and shut easily.

To make the front door open well, outwards, the hinge line of the door (KK) should be half cut through on the inside. The hinge can be strengthened by gumming a narrow strip of paper or linen along it. At the three points marked G make small slits through which to put the tags, also marked G, of the partition wall.

All drawing and painting must be done on both sides while the house is still flat. The doors inside will need handles and keyholes. Small pieces of mica can be gummed over the windows instead of glass.

Little curtains of crinkly tissue-paper can also be made, and, if you like, the walls can easily be papered with coloured paper pasted on. This will cause some delay, however, for it must be well pressed. Instead, wall-paper patterns could be painted on.

Outside—that is, on the underside of the cardboard—there is a great deal to do. Both walls and roof can be painted, and tiles, bricks, and creepers imitated. The front door should have a knocker and a letter-box, and around both the door and the windows should be imitation framework. As the upright joints of the four walls will be made of stamp-paper or linen painted to imitate brick-work or stone-work, you need not carry the painting of the walls quite to the edges, because these will be covered by the joints. It is best to paint the joints before you stick them on.

Before turning the card over again, run your knife along the four sides of the floor to assist the bending up of the walls. Do not on any account cut through ; merely make a half cut.

When you have drawn and painted all you can think of to make the house complete and pretty, take your strips of stamp-paper or linen, for the fastening of the walls, crease them in half, lengthwise, and gum one half to the outside of the edge of the

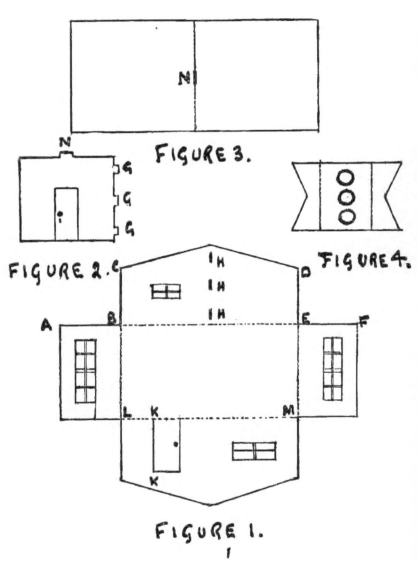

FIGURE 3.

FIGURE 4.

FIGURE 2.

FIGURE 1.

CARDBOARD DOLLS' HOUSE.

walls marked CB and DE in the plan. When this is quite dry, bend the back wall and the two side walls up, and gum the free sides of the strips to the wall marked AB and EF, holding the walls firmly together until well stuck. Strengthen the fold LM, which has to serve as a hinge for the front of the house, with a strip of linen gummed underneath. The sides of the front wall must remain unattached, as that forms the opening. It can be kept closed by a strong pin slipped through the roof.

APPEARANCE OF HOUSE WHEN COMPLETE.

tion.

Now for the partition. Put the three tags G G G through the slits H H H and gum them firmly down on the outside. (These will have to be touched up with paint.) The roof must then be put on. Cut out a slit N an inch long to fit the tag on the partition, also marked N. Run your knife along the dotted line underneath, and fold it to the necessary angle to fit the sloping walls. Where the roof touches the end walls it must be fastened on with strips of linen or paper, which have been folded in the same way as before and one half fastened securely to the walls. It is important to let it get quite dry before gumming the other half to the roof.

20

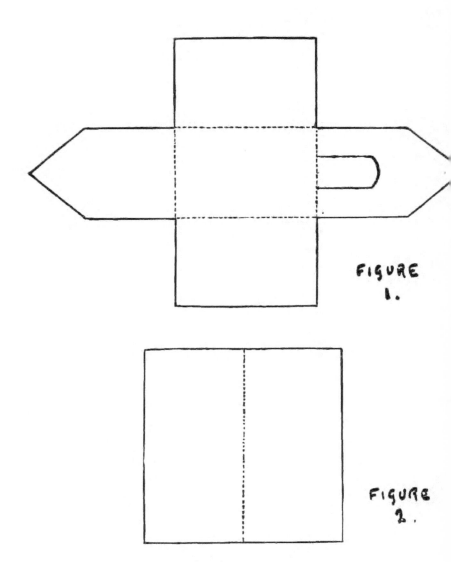

FIGURE
1.

FIGURE
2.

DOG-KENNEL (Fig. 1) AND ROOF (Fig. 2).

The chimney, of which the illustration is the actual size, is the last thing to be made. First paint, and then fold the two side pieces downwards, cut out the three little holes and put into them three chimneys, made by folding small pieces of paper, painted red, round a penholder, and gumming their edges together. The chimney is fixed to the sloping roof with very small pieces of gummed paper. Remember that all the pieces of paper used as fastening ought to be touched up with paint. The chimney in the drawing of the complete house on page 196 is put at the side of the roof, but it may even better go in the middle.

The cottage can then be fixed to a piece of wood or pasteboard, to form its garden and add to convenience in moving it about. A cardboard fence and gate can be cut out and painted green. A path to the front door is made by covering a narrow space of the cardboard with very thin gum over which, while it is wet, sand is sprinkled to imitate gravel. Moss will do for evergreens, and grass plots can be made of green cloth. A summer-house, garden chairs and tables are easily cut out of cardboard. So also are a rabbit-hutch, pump, dove-cot, and dog-kennel. A plan of a dog-kennel, actual size, is given.

It is, of course, possible to make a house of several pieces instead of one. The walls and floors can be made separately and joined with linen strips ; but this adds to the difficulty of the work and causes the house to be less steady. Cardboard houses can also be made with two floors.

PAPER FURNITURE

Everything required for the furnishing and peopling of a cardboard dolls' house can be made of paper ; and if coloured at all cleverly the furniture will appear to be as solid as that of wood. After cutting out and joining together one or two of the models given in the pages that follow, and thus learning the principle on which paper furniture is made, you will be able to add all kinds of things to those mentioned here or to devise new patterns for old articles, such as chairs and desks.

Two recent inventions of the greatest possible use to the maker of paper furniture are seccotine, a kind of gum which gets dry very quickly and is more than ordinarily strong, and adhesive tape. Seccotine can be bought for a penny a tube, and adhesive tape, which is sold principally for mending music and the torn pages of books, is put up in penny reels.

Seccotir and adh tape.

A pair of compasses is a good thing to have ; but you can make a perfectly serviceable tool by cutting out a narrow strip of cardboard about four inches long and boring holes at intervals of a quarter of an inch, through which the point of a pencil can be placed. If one end of the strip is fastened to the paper with a pin you can draw a circle of what size you want, up to eight inches across.

Home-m compass

These are the materials needed when making paper furniture:— *Materi*

A few sheets of stiff note-paper or drawing-paper.   Scissors.   A penknife A ruler (a flat penny one).   A mapping-pen.   A box of paints.   A board to cut out on.   Adhesive tape (a 1d. reel) or stamp-paper.   Seccotine (a 1d. tube).

If the drawings are to be traced, tracing-paper, or transparent *Tracing* note-paper, and a sheet of carbon-paper, will also be needed. To trace a drawing, cover it with paper and draw it exactly. Then cover the paper or cardboard from which you wish to cut out the furniture with a piece of carbon-paper, black side down, and over that place your tracing. Draw over this again with a very sharply pointed pencil or pointed stick, and the lines will be repeated by the carbon-paper on the under sheet of paper.

The furniture, for which designs are given in this chapter, can be made of stiff note-paper, Whatman's drawing-paper, or thin Bristol board. The drawings can be copied or traced. In either case the greatest care must be taken that the measurements are minutely correct and the lines perfectly straight. A slip of paper is a very good thing to measure with.

Enough designs have been given to show how most different

kinds of furniture can be made. These can, of course, be varied and increased by copying from good furniture lists; while many little things such as saucepans, dishes, clocks, and so forth, can be copied from stores lists and added to the few that are given below and on p. 203.

These small articles are cut out flat, but an extra piece of paper is left under each, which, when bent back, makes a stand.

THREE CARDBOARD UTENSILS.

al
ctions. The front legs of chairs, the legs of tables, and the backs of furniture must be neatly joined together by narrow strips of stamp-paper or adhesive tape. To do this, cut a strip of the right size crease it down the middle, and stick one side. Allow this to dry, before you fix the other.

Wherever in the pictures there is a dotted line, it means that the paper is to be folded there. It will be easily seen whether it is to be folded up or down.

Before the furniture is folded it should be painted. Wood, iron, brass, and silk can all be imitated in colour.

In cutting out small spaces of cardboard—as between the bars of a chair—lay the card on a board, and keeping your knife, which should be sharp at the point, against a flat ruler, run it again and again along the lines you want to cut, until you have cut through. If your furniture is made of paper, the spaces can be cut out with finely pointed scissors, taking care to start in the middle of the space, for the first incision is seldom a clean one.

24

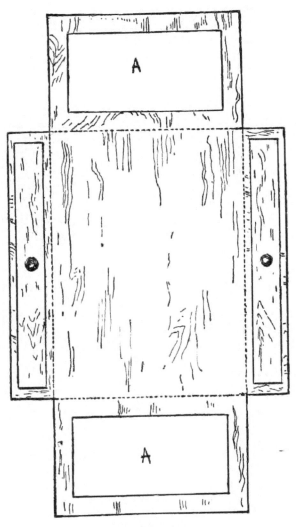

KITCHEN TABLE.

(Cut out the oblong parts marked A.)

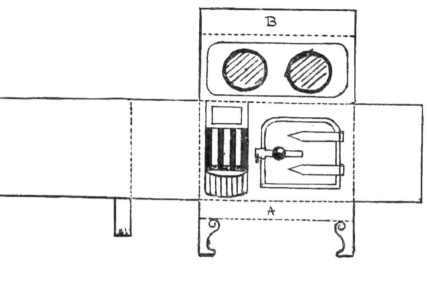

KITCHEN RANGE AND KITCHEN CHAIR.

A is turned up to form a shelf for saucepans.   B is gummed down over the back.)

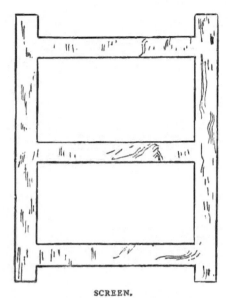

SCREEN.

(To be made of one piece of paper folded into three equal parts and cut out in accordance with the illustration.)

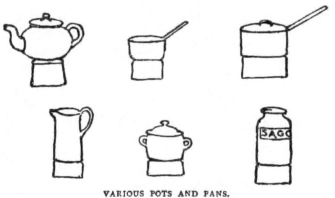

VARIOUS POTS AND PANS.

(Under part to be folded back for a stand)

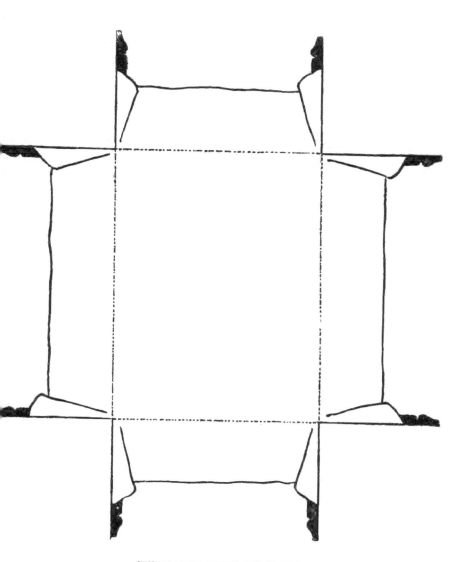

DINING-ROOM TABLE AND CLOTH.

28

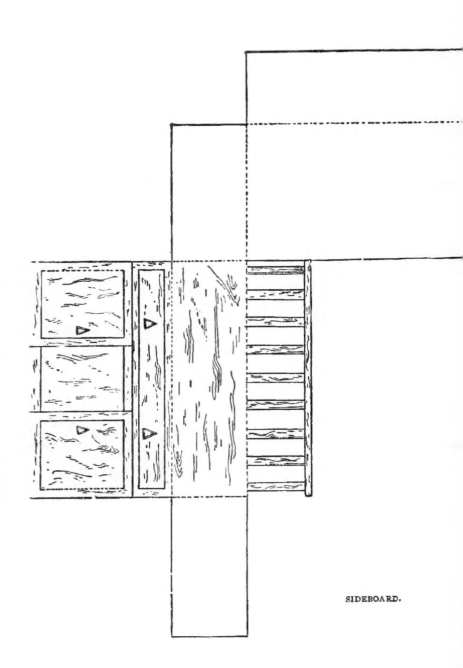

SIDEBOARD.

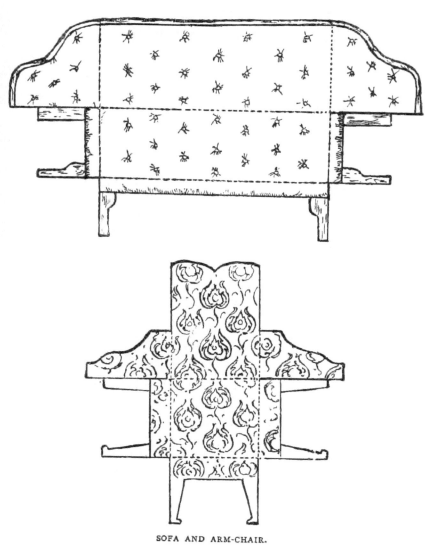

SOFA AND ARM-CHAIR.

(The corners must be fastened to the seat by very narrow strips of paper.)

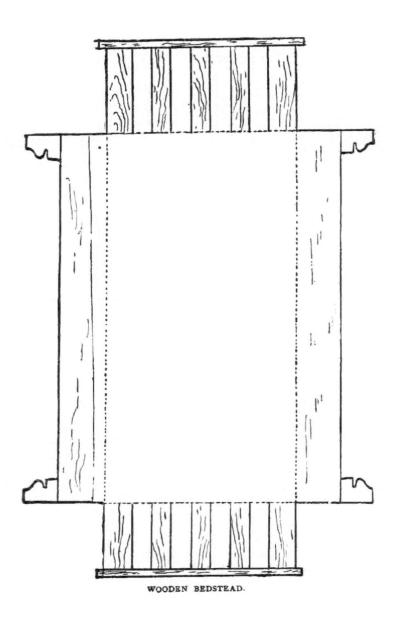

WOODEN BEDSTEAD.

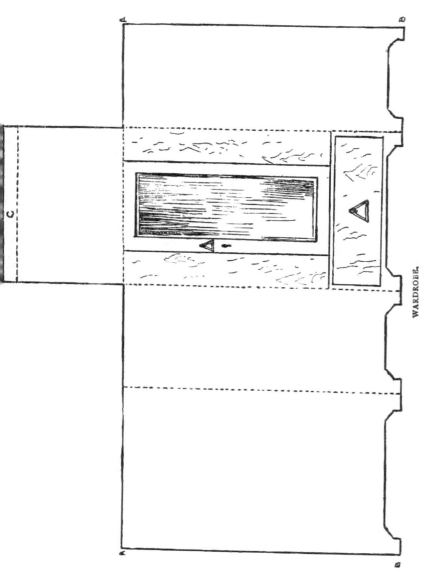

WARDROBE.

(Join the sides AB and AB, and then bend the top down, gumming the extra flap C on to the back of the wardrobe.)

32

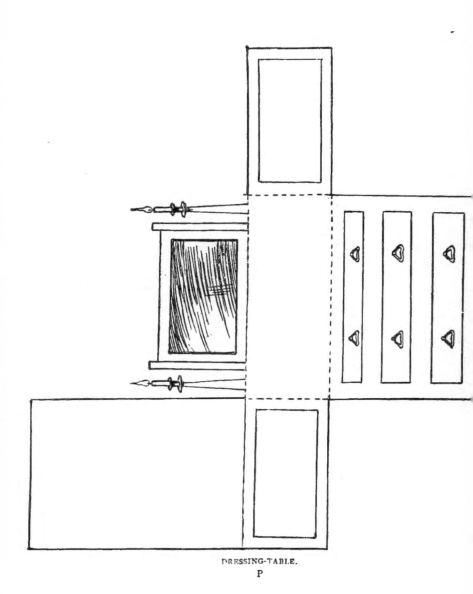

DRESSING-TABLE.

P

33

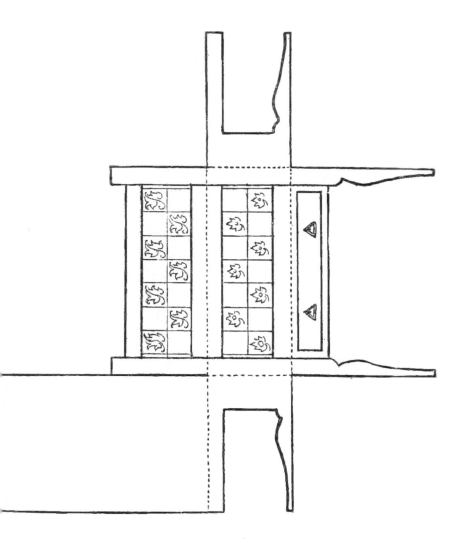

WASH-HAND STAND.

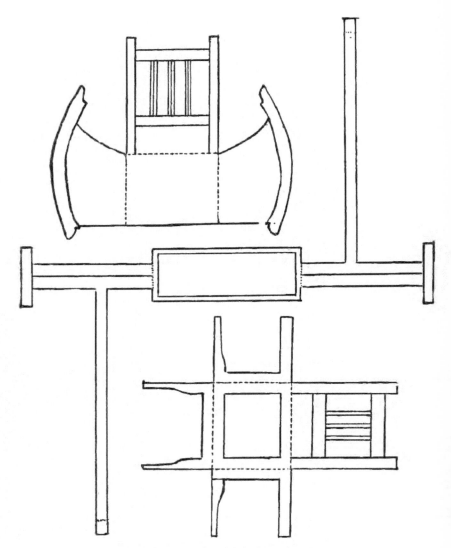

ROCKING-CHAIR, TOWEL-HORSE, AND CHAIR.

35

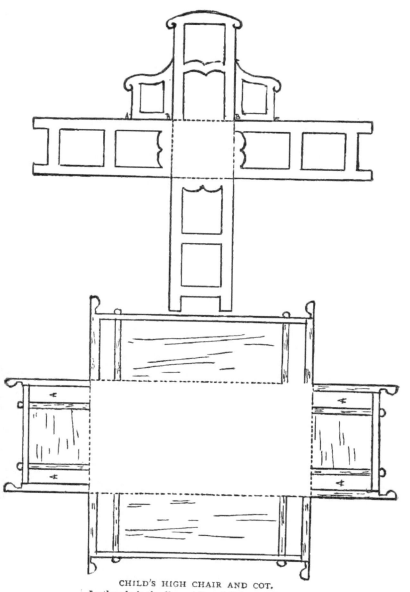

CHILD'S HIGH CHAIR AND COT.
In the chair the lines AB and BA must be cut.
the cot the four pieces marked A are cut out on three sides and bent down to form legs.

PAPER DOLLS

Paper dolls are not as good to play with as proper dolls. One can do much less with them because they cannot be washed, have no hair to be brushed, and should not sit down. But they can be exceedingly pretty, and the keeping of their wardrobes in touch with the fashion is an absorbing occupation. Paper dolls are more interesting to those who like painting than to others. The pleasure of colouring them and their dresses is to many of us quite as interesting as cutting out and sewing the clothes of ordinary dolls.

The first thing to do is to draw the doll in pencil on the *Making* cardboard or paper which it is to be cut from. If you are not *paper doll* good at drawing, the best way is to trace a figure in a book or newspaper, and then, slipping a piece of carbon-paper (which can be bought for a penny or less at any stationer's) between your tracing-paper and the cardboard, to go over the outline again with a pencil or a pointed stick. On uncovering the cardboard you will find the doll there all ready to cut out. It should then be coloured on both sides, partly flesh colour and partly underclothes.

The dresses are made of sheets of notepaper, the fold of which *The dress* forms the shoulder pieces. The doll is laid on the paper, with head and neck lapping over the fold, and the line of the dress is then drawn a little larger than the doll. A small round nick to form the collar is cut between the shoulders of the dress, and a slit is made down the back through which the doll's head can be passed. After the head is through it is turned round. (Of course, if the dress is for evening the place which you cut for the neck must be larger, and in this case no slit will be needed.) All the details of the dresses, which can be of original design, or copied from advertisements and fashion plates, must be drawn in in pencil and afterwards painted. Hats, trimmed with tissue-paper feathers or ribbons, are made of round pieces of notepaper with a slit in them just big enough for the tip of the doll's head to go

PAPER MOTHER AND CHILD, WITH CLOTHES FOR EACH.
(Designed and made by Miss S. M. Clayton.)

A PAPER GIRL, WITH SIX CHANGES.
(Designed and made by Miss M. C. G. Jackson.)

through.   The illustrations on pp. 214 and 215 should make
everything clear.

ue-paper   Dresses can also be made of crinkly tissue-paper gummed to
es.   a foundation of plain notepaper.   Frills, flounces, and sashes are
easily imitated in this material, and if the colours are well chosen
the result is very pretty.

r paper   Simpler and absolutely symmetrical paper dolls are made by
cutting them out of folded paper, so that the fold runs right

WALKING PAPER DOLLS.

down the middle of the doll.   By folding many pieces of paper
together, one can cut out many dolls at once.

king   Walking ladies are made in that way ; but they must have
long skirts and no feet, and when finished a cut is made in the
skirt—as in the picture—and the framework thus produced is
bent back.   When the doll is placed on the table and gently
blown it will move gracefully along.

s of   To make a row of paper dolls, take a piece of paper the height
r dolls. that the dolls are to be, and fold it alternately backwards and
forwards (first one side and then the other) leaving about an inch

40

between each fold. Press the folds together tightly and cut out the half of a doll, being careful that the arms are continued to the edge of the fold and are not cut off. Open out and you will have a string of paper dolls.

Lightning Source UK Ltd.
Milton Keynes UK
UKHW040854110320
360160UK00002B/362